How to

Succeed in Your First Job

How to
Succeed in
Your First Job

Tips for New College Graduates

Elwood F. Holton III

Sharon S. Naquin

BK

BERRETT-KOEHLER PUBLISHERS, INC.
San Francisco

Berrett-Koehler Publishers, Inc.
235 Montgomery Street, Suite 650
San Francisco, CA 94104-2916
Tel: (415) 288-0260   Fax: (415) 362-2512 www.bkconnection.com

Ordering Information
Quantity sales. Special discounts are available on quantity purchases by corporations, associations, and others. For details, contact the "Special Sales Department" at the Berrett-Koehler address above.

Individual sales. Berrett-Koehler publications are available through most bookstores. They can also be ordered directly from Berrett-Koehler: Tel: (800) 929-2929; Fax: (802) 864-7626; www.bkconnection.com

Orders for college textbook/course adoption use. Please contact Berrett-Koehler: Tel: (800) 929-2929; Fax: (802) 864-7626.

Orders by U.S. trade bookstores and wholesalers. Please contact Publishers Group West, 1700 Fourth Street, Berkeley, CA 94710. Tel: (510) 528-1444; Fax (510) 528-3444.

Berrett-Koehler and the BK logo are registered trademarks of Berrett-Koehler Publishers, Inc.

Printed in the United States of America

Berrett-Koehler books are printed on long-lasting acid-free paper. When it is available, we choose paper that has been manufactured by environmentally responsible processes. These may include using trees grown in sustainable forests, incorporating recycled paper, minimizing chlorine in bleaching, or recycling the energy produced at the paper mill.

Library of Congress Cataloging-in-Publication Data

Holton, Ed., 1957–
   How to succeed in your first job: tips for new college graduates / Elwood F. Holton III, Sharon S. Naquin
      p.   cm.
      ISBN-10: 1-58376-166-7; ISBN-13: 978-1-58376-166-3
   1. Vocational guidance—United States. 2. College graduates—Employment—United States. I. Naquin, Sharon S. II. Title.
   HF5382.5.U5 H627 2000
      650.14'084'2—dc21   00-011216

First Edition
12 11 10 09 08 07 06   10 9 8 7 6 5 4 3

Cover and Interior Design: Bookwrights Design
Editorial Services: PeopleSpeak
Indexing: Directions Unlimited

To our children:

Blair Naquin
And
Karie and Melanie Holton
May your lives be filled with happiness and success,
however you choose to define the two.

Contents

Preface   ix

One   The Art of Being New   **1**
Two   What College Failed to Teach You   **6**
Three   Step 1: Adopt the Right Attitudes   **14**
Four   Step 2: Adjust Your Expectations   **19**
Five   Step 3: Master Breaking-in Skills   **21**
Six   Step 4: Manage the Impressions You Make   **25**
Seven   Step 5: Build Effective Relationships   **28**
Eight   Step 6: Become a Good Follower   **32**
Nine   Step 7: Understand Your Organization's
            Culture   **36**
Ten   Step 8: Adapt to the Organizational System   **39**
Eleven   Step 9: Understand Your New-Hire Role   **42**
Twelve   Step 10: Develop Work Smarts   **46**
Thirteen   Step 11: Master the Tasks of Your Job   **49**
Fourteen   Step 12: Acquire the Knowledge, Skills, and
            Abilities You Need   **51**
Fifteen   Taking Responsibility for Your First-Year
            Success   **53**
Sixteen   The Quick-Start Learning Tool   **57**

Conclusion: Get on the "Success Spiral"   **67**
Appendix A: Quick-Start Learning Templates   **69**
Appendix B: Quick-Start Personal Action Plan   **78**
Index   **80**
Related Books   **84**
About the Authors **85**

Preface

Over the years we have counseled, taught, and coached many college students and new college graduates on career issues. We have also hired many college students and college graduates. While there are many success stories, we have also seen so many instances where new graduates and their companies made mistake after mistake. We have always thought "there must be a better way" to do this. This book arose out of our conviction to find a way to help. Furthermore, we both vividly remember our own confusing experiences as new college graduates entering the work world. We wrote the book we wish someone had given us when we started work.

Over the past twelve years we have used the twelve-step process in this book to coach countless new employees on how to make a better start in their careers. The really good news is that, for most, learning a better way to start their careers was a personal relief and a boost to their careers. We know this system works. Our challenge in this book was to package our advice in a concise, user-friendly format so readers could quickly access the system for today's hurry-up world.

As we will discuss in the book, our research shows that college has not prepared you to become an effective professional like you think it has. College only prepares you for certain aspects of the job. We encourage you to be open-minded as you read so you can learn some new skills to help you start your career. Both research and experience tells us that what you don't know about starting your career can have a huge, detrimental effect on your success. A little time invested here can make the transition from college to work easier and more successful.

Best wishes for a great start to your career!

Elwood F. Holton III
Sharon S. Naquin
Baton Rouge, Louisiana

One

The Art of Being New

John didn't know.

"I'm really stunned," said John, a new college graduate beginning his second month of work with a major corporation. He had just had a meeting with his boss and was discussing it with a fellow new hire. "I really thought I was doing well. During my first week I found a mistake my project engineer had made. Then in the staff meeting last week, I spent twenty minutes talking about a new technique I learned in school that could be helpful. In the meeting with the vice president, I was careful to keep quiet and let my boss do the talking. Now she tells me I'm too cocky, my attitude is irritating others, and I need to be more of a team player. And the vice president thinks I'm a wimp. I was only trying to do my best to help. Where did I go wrong? Why didn't my boss tell me earlier what I was supposed to be doing?"

Every year, thousands of college students all over the country work hard at planning their careers, honing their interview and resume-writing skills, and preparing for their job searches. Many find good jobs and start work with high enthusiasm and energy, only to be disappointed in the results. Why? Because most of them overlook a critical step, which makes much of the hard work that went into finding a job worthless. Like John, they haven't learned how to make the transition from college to work.

Does that sound a little strange? You just graduate and go to work, right? Far from it—although you might assume exactly that. Most managers and executives we interviewed complained that new graduates just don't understand what it takes to successfully enter a new organization.

This book is designed to help you understand *what* you need to learn during your first year on the job and *how* to learn it. The book addresses the first purpose by discussing the transition to work and the skills you must acquire. It also provides an interview protocol to help you collect the information you need from others in your organization, a set of analysis forms to help you interpret what people tell you, and planning sheets for you to map out your development. Complete worksheets can also be downloaded from our Web site: www.NewEmployeeSuccess.com.

The book is built around a core twelve-step process for new employees entering an organization. This model is firmly grounded in fifteen years of research and field-testing but is presented in a user-friendly, practical format. The model has been developed and refined through numerous presentations to new employee and human resource practitioner groups and through consulting engagements in organizations such as J. P. Morgan, Enterprise Rent-A-Car, the U.S. Department of Energy, the U.S. General Services Administration, and the Multiple Sclerosis Society.

The Unique First Year

Starting to work in an organization is a unique and critically important event that requires a special perspective and special strategies for success. You need to recognize that the first year on a new job is a separate and distinct career stage. It is a transition stage; you're not a college student anymore, but— this may surprise you—you're not really a professional yet either. If you consider the first year on the job separately from the rest of the career ladder, the world of work will begin to make sense.

Wise graduates know that many new graduates hang on to their college student attitudes and behaviors too long. But few realize that it also takes time to earn the rights, responsibilities, and credibility of a full-fledged professional. An intermediate stage lasts from the time you accept your first job after graduation until about the end of the first year. This stage might make or break the early part of your career.

You must follow a different set of guidelines during this transition period, or breaking-in stage. Because you are the newcomer—the "outsider" in the minds of your coworkers—people will respond to you differently, work with you differently, and judge you differently from others. You, in response, have to approach them differently. Special dynamics occur during the first year, and most graduates aren't given the new guidelines. That was John's problem in the earlier scenario: he didn't understand that only by learning new guidelines could he have a strong start in his career.

Learning the new rules is essential to a fast career start, yet few new graduates take the time to do so and they start their jobs all wrong. If you are a wise new employee, you'll recognize this as a golden opportunity to distinguish yourself from other new hires and excel by showing your professional maturity.

Does It Really Matter?

Does this stage really matter? You're absolutely right it does. The way in which you enter a new job with an organization will have a major impact on your success within that organization. Much of your early career opportunity and success will depend on the impressions you make on the people you work with and the perceptions they develop of you in the early weeks and months on the job. Research suggests that how you approach your first year will have a major impact on your future salary, advancement, job satisfaction, and ability to move within the organization, as well as your own feelings of success and commitment to the job. And it can impact your career for many years to come.

Your challenge in the early months will be to use the strategies in this book to establish your reputation as a bright, capable, and valuable employee and to earn the respect of your colleagues. If you are successful, you will quickly be given opportunities to make a real contribution to the company and to make yourself visible to upper management. If you then take advantage of those early opportunities by demonstrating what an outstanding performer you are, more opportunities to succeed will follow. Edgar Schein, a noted management author, called this the "success spiral," and you want to get on it!

Miss the opportunity to prove yourself and you may find yourself labeled as "immature" and relegated to lesser assignments while your colleagues—and competitors for promotions—are busy impressing the boss with their professional maturity and success on good assignments. Do you really want to give your competitors a head start? That's not to say that an entire thirty-year career is made or broken in a few months' performance. However, the simple fact is that it can take years to recover from a poor start.

Two

What College Failed to Teach You

You probably know that college is a special world, but you won't know how different it is until you start to work. At the heart of the problems most new graduates (and their managers) experience during their transition is the failure to recognize how much the educational culture has shaped their attitudes, expectations, behaviors, and overall view of the organizations for which they choose to work. Think about it. You have spent at least seventeen years in an educational setting. How could that not shape you?

This may sound a little simplistic, but the effects of living in an educational culture for so long are more powerful than you think. When we conduct workshops for new graduates after they have been at work for about six months, we ask them to list their work-related frustrations. We put these lists on flip charts along one wall. Then we ask them to recall what college was like for them and put those lists on the opposite wall. The "aha" that they experience is that 80 to 90 percent of their complaints are either caused by or greatly exacerbated by their failure to recognize and let go of their deeply ingrained college-learned attitudes, expectations, and behaviors. They are always shocked to see how powerful the influence of college is, even though they thought they fully understood that college and work are different.

You may also be surprised to discover that the skills you learned in order to be a successful student (e.g., getting along with teachers, doing class projects) and the behaviors for which you were rewarded are rarely the ones you'll need to be successful at work! College and work are fundamentally different. The *knowledge* you acquired in college will be critical to your success, but the *process* of succeeding in school is very different from the process of succeeding at work. Certain aspects of your education may have prepared you to be a professional, but evidence from the workplace indicates that this is not enough for professional success.

For example, if you majored in accounting, the accounting principles you learned will be invaluable to you. But most likely, you didn't learn all the professional skills you need to be a good public accountant (e.g., interfacing with clients and attorneys, working well with project teams, selling ideas to managing partners). Worse yet, the culture of education is so different from the culture of work that if you continue to have the same expectations of your employer that you did of your college and professors, you'll be greatly disappointed with your job and make costly career mistakes. By taking the time to learn the culture of work and what it means to be a professional, you'll avoid making a fool of yourself by taking classroom behavior into the workplace (like John).

These are some of the key differences that new graduates talk about:

COLLEGE	FIRST YEAR OF WORK
Frequent, quick, and concrete feedback (grades, etc.)	Infrequent and less precise feedback
Highly structured curriculum and programs with lots of direction	Highly unstructured environment and tasks with little direction
Few significant changes	Frequent and unexpected changes
Flexible schedule	Structured schedule
Frequent breaks and time off	Limited time off
Personal control over time, classes, interests	Need to respond to others' directions and interests
Intellectual challenge	Organizational and people challenges
Choice of performance level ("A," "B," etc.)	"A"-level work always required
Focus on personal development and growth	Focus on getting results for the organization
Opportunity to create and explore knowledge	Expectation to get results with one's knowledge
Individual effort	Team effort
"Right" answers	Few "right" answers
Independence of ideas and thinking	"Do it the company's way"
Professors	Bosses
Less initiative required	Lots of initiative required

Let's look at a few examples of how failing to recognize these differences can hurt you:

- In college, you usually received a lot of direction about what to do and how to do it. Your major's curriculum dictated most of your courses, and your professors told you what was expected. If a professor didn't give you a clear syllabus or tell you what to study for an exam, chances are you probably got upset. At work, you'll rarely get the same type of direction. But you've become so accustomed to receiving it that you may well complain that your manager won't tell you what to do.

- Your college education has taught you how to argue your position to convince a professor that you are right and he or she is wrong. Classroom discussions frequently become philosophical debates with no clear winners or losers. Tact and diplomacy are often replaced with passion and insistence. If you try that approach with your boss in a meeting, it won't be received well.

- Your college experience has made you so accustomed to being frequently told "how you're doing" that you might expect the same kind of constant feedback from your manager. However, if you persistently seek feedback from your manager, you run the risk of leaving the impression that you are insecure.

- Some new graduates are so used to growing and developing through education that they get very upset when their bosses won't send them to enough training classes during the first year. They forget that organizations expect some periods of productivity interspersed with training.

- Still others can't understand why they aren't getting to do work that stretches their minds and challenges them. They don't realize that work will never mimic college.

"Not me," you say? That's not necessarily true. You will make mistakes like these simply out of habit if you're not careful. You shouldn't just do what comes naturally; what comes naturally is what you've done for the last seventeen years—act like a student. You may think you know how to act like a professional, but nearly every student will automatically react to the workplace as if it were an educational institution. These studentlike behaviors, which you may not even realize you are maintaining, will cause you to be labeled "naive" and "immature." It takes lots of effort to let go of those old ways and accept the institution of work for what it is—different. But this is the key to a successful first year. Can you let go, or will you insist on holding on to old ways? It's your decision.

What's Really Important in the First Year?

If you are like most new graduates, you're probably thinking a lot about the tasks you've been hired to do. What wonderful challenges! You will finally be able to put those long years of study to actual use, and you'll have exciting opportunities to develop your abilities as you tackle these new challenges. You may also feel insecure, a bit worried and anxious about your abilities. "Do I have what it takes to be successful at these challenges?" "Do I know enough to compete?" "Am I good enough to do the job?" These are all questions you may ask yourself.

Guess what your employer is worried about? It's not your ability to do your job tasks. Rather, your employer is concerned about your ability to do the nontask components of the job. These include your willingness and ability to learn new ideas,

10

fit into the company's culture, earn respect and credibility, learn the politics of the organization, build effective working relationships, become an accepted member of the organization, learn the informal structure and methods of the company, discover what the unwritten expectations are, understand the power-and-reward structure, and learn how to accomplish work within the organization.

Most employers (particularly large ones) are very adept at hiring people whom they believe have the raw talent and ability to perform the basic tasks of their jobs. Yet many new graduates feel that is exactly what they have to prove. When managers of new employees are asked what makes the difference between an average new employee and an outstanding new employee, task performance has little to do with the answers. Outstanding new employees, they say, are the ones who have good attitudes, get along with people, learn about the organization quickly, fit in, and exhibit other characteristics we will discuss here. Performing the basic tasks of your job well will earn you only an average performance rating.

The conclusion is that most new graduates are focused on the wrong elements of a job: task-related knowledge and skills. Why? Because these are what college focuses on. The twelve steps outlined below will help you focus on what your employer is actually concerned about: the nontask elements of your job. If you want to be more than just an average performer, you will need to shift your focus.

First-Year Goals

Your goals for the first year have to include more than just productivity. Equally important are three other goals: earning *acceptance,* earning *respect,* and earning *credibility.*

11

Organizations are groups of people, and just because you have been hired does not mean that you have been accepted by those people as "one of them." Acceptance is earned, as are respect and credibility. Your colleagues will not automatically respect you, your expertise, or the contributions you make. Although your success in college enabled you to be hired, it, by itself, is not enough on the job. You have to prove yourself all over again.

In fact, because you are a new college graduate, your co-workers may be biased against you since you are so inexperienced. You will have to convince them that you are professionally mature and deserving of their respect. Only then will anyone consider your expertise, experiences, and contributions credible and worthwhile.

Overview of the Twelve-Step Process

Now let's discuss specifically what you should learn. A twelve-step process that presents the key developmental tasks for new employees entering an organization serves as a guide for this section. The steps, grouped into four areas, are listed below:

Individual Focus

Step 1: Adopt the right attitudes.

Step 2: Adjust your expectations.

Step 3: Master breaking-in skills.

People Focus

Step 4: Manage the impressions you make.

Step 5: Build effective relationships.

Step 6: Become a good follower.

Organization Focus

Step 7:   Understand your organization's culture.

Step 8:   Adapt to the organizational system.

Step 9:   Understand the art of being new.

Work Task Focus

Step 10:   Develop work smarts.

Step 11:   Master the tasks of your job.

Step 12:   Acquire the knowledge, skills, and abilities
you need.

The first nine steps of this twelve-step process will help you accomplish your three first-year goals and prepare you to do your job tasks well. The last three steps are task-related; they complete the process and enable you to be productive. By taking the first nine steps, you will demonstrate your professional maturity, become accepted and respected in your organization, and learn how business is done. Then, and only then, can you achieve outstanding performance on the tasks of your job.

Surprised that the task-related steps are last? Make no mistake, you must be proficient at the tasks you are asked to perform. But becoming an outstanding employee—which should be your overall goal—requires much more than technical skill or know-how. No matter how brilliant you are or how successful you have been in school, it is nearly impossible for you to receive an outstanding performance rating at the end of your first year without first mastering the nontask aspects of your job. Why? Because getting results (remember, results are what count) in whatever tasks you are assigned will require you to work with other people and within an organizational system. And you can't really understand the task until you understand the people and the organization.

Three

Step 1: Adopt the Right Attitudes

E mployers' number one complaint is about the attitude new graduates bring to the workplace. Your challenge is to identify "success-related attitudes." Look around and find people in the organization who seem successful and respected by others. What are their attitudes toward other people, their jobs, the organization, and the future of the organization? Try to develop similar attitudes yourself.

Here are some key attitudes and characteristics that managers in almost every organization say new graduates need to develop.

Humility

Your graduation from college can leave you with a false sense of importance and capability. You have a right to be proud

14

of what you have accomplished and to be confident, but college has given you only a foundation. You have another degree to earn, and your new major is the realities of the world of work. The two worlds are that different.

Some of the graduates who struggle the most with the transition are those who have been campus leaders or academic successes. Consider Mary, the student government association president, who was accustomed to running meetings, setting agendas, interfacing directly with high-ranking campus administrators, and being able to "make things happen." In her first job after college, she was suddenly the lowest ranking member of the team, with little or no authority and few privileges. She initially fought against the constraints of her new role and attempted to assume her old role as the one who called the shots, particularly in meetings. However, she was quickly humbled by the negative reaction she received from her boss and colleagues. Had she not learned to keep her naturally assertive behavior in check until she gained more experience, she certainly would have alienated herself within her organization and would have been labeled as arrogant and bossy.

Readiness for continual learning

It's not how much you know that is most important to your employer, but rather your understanding of how much you have yet to learn and your willingness to learn it. Seize every opportunity you can to learn. If work is a little slow around the office, then study something. Take your training seriously. Ask questions before you tell someone what you think the answer is regarding a problem you see. Don't resist when your previous learning is challenged. Your colleagues know you are smart; now show them you can learn.

Readiness to change

Graduate after graduate complains that life at work "isn't what they told me it would be." Organizational life is full of changes, and new graduates need to be flexible. Be aware that colleges are designed to resist change, whereas business organizations try to respond to change. A flexible and adaptive attitude wins points.

Respect

Your organization is the way it is and works the way it does for some reason. Few organizations are perfect, but you must respect yours for what it is before you criticize it. If you want the people in your organization to respect you and your knowledge and contributions, you have to give them respect first.

Confidence

Employers want to see confidence—but the right kind. What earns respect is confidence about your *potential* combined with humility about your newness and lack of organizational awareness. Be proud of what you have achieved but realistic about what you can do now. Joel, for instance, mistakenly assumed that his ability to design an award-winning architectural model as a senior project made him the natural choice as a key architect in the design of a $300-million office complex. However, his confidence looked like foolish overconfidence to his more experienced colleagues. Instead of assuming he would have a key role, Joel would have been more respected if he had recognized that the skills he learned in college would enable him to provide much-needed assistance on the project.

Open-mindedness

The worst thing you can bring to the job is a preconceived notion about what work ought to be like, how it ought to be done, and what you are supposed to do. Start with an open mind about the organization and its way of doing business. Be amenable to new ways of thinking and working and be open to new experiences.

Longer-term perspective

Your first year is really a time to lay a foundation for the future. Your employer probably views your development as occurring over several years, not just a few months. New graduates, on the other hand, are typically more shortsighted. College students have been conditioned to taking courses that last from just six to fifteen weeks. However, a successful professional's attitude is one that says, "I'm here for the long haul, and being rewarded for what I'm doing today or even this month is not as important as how my efforts are preparing me for future success." People with this attitude willingly accept assignments that aren't fun but are good training. Even though long-term employment relationships are no longer the norm, most college graduates' time horizons are still too short for the workplace.

Strong work ethic

Don't skip this item or minimize its importance! We haven't met a graduate yet who didn't think he or she was a hard worker, but employers often don't agree. Many graduates find that professional life is a lot more demanding than college. Employers often complain that graduates aren't ready to work hard. Is this an overgeneralization? Maybe, but heed this advice: show up early, stay late, volunteer for projects, and work extra hard at learning. The differences between college and work make the first year on the job a lot harder than subsequent years. Therefore, extra effort is called for and gets noticed. Go the "extra mile" and do whatever is asked—no matter how trivial the task seems to you.

Positive attitude

In college, complaining is pretty common. Whether it is about the professors, dumb assignments, the lousy administration, or the workload, almost everyone does it. However, your employer wants to see a positive attitude—not a complaining, negative one. Complaining isn't acceptable when you are new, even though older employees may do it. Resist the temptation to join in "gripe sessions" with your coworkers. Such patterns are unhealthy and will hurt you far more than any benefit you might expect to gain by venting. Negativity is seductive but destructive.

Four

Step 2: Adjust Your Expectations

N ew graduates' expectations are a major cause of the frustration experienced in the first year on the job. The frustration you may experience is nothing more than the difference between expectations and reality. If you keep your expectations realistic, you won't be disappointed. Expect to be surprised because the odds are that many aspects of your job will be different from what you think they will be.

It's important to realize that the image the organization's recruiter painted may have been a bit too rosy and that you won't receive the special attention from others in the organization that you did while being recruited. The reality of your first job is that it probably won't be nearly as glamorous, important, or high level as you may expect. Most employers are very frustrated with the expectations of new graduates, so you'll impress others if you work to keep yours realistic. For instance, you can't always expect your coworkers to drop what they are doing to help you. In addition, the way decisions are made won't be as logical as you expect because of office politics. People skills and teamwork will be much more important than you probably ever imagined. New graduates often comment on how different the challenges, the pressure they feel, the hours they work, and the kinds of tasks they perform are from what they expected.

Your expectations are where the college experience has shaped you—and hurt you—the most. If you find yourself frustrated and having any of the following thoughts, you're probably expecting work to be too much like college:

- "I never really know how well I'm doing."

- "Work is boring."

- "Things aren't like the recruiter said they would be."

- "Nobody tells me what I'm supposed to do."

- "If the managers were really interested in me they would help me."

- "Nobody will tell me how things work around here."

- "The managers keep changing their minds."

- "This is just grunt work; it's beneath me."

- "My coworkers don't want my new ideas."

While these frustrations could also be symptoms of real problems, in your first year they are more than likely the result of student thinking. Start with a "clean slate."

Five

Step 3: Master Breaking-in Skills

W e've already stated that different guidelines apply to your first year on the job. We call these "breaking-in" skills. Let's look at some more basics about being a successful newcomer.

You are an outsider until you prove otherwise

This is a fundamental fact that you must remember at all times. Just because you are being paid by your organization does not mean that the people in the organization have accepted you. Becoming accepted within the organization is your responsibility.

You can't change the system until you are part of it

New graduates are particularly likely to want to implement some of the ideas they've learned in college. They often bring a fresh perspective to an organization and can spot opportunities for improvement that other employees can't. But suggestions for change and improvement imply that the current system is flawed in some way. Be careful. When an insider criticizes the organization or tries to make changes, it is considered constructive. When an outsider (that's you) criticizes or suggests changes, this probably will be seen as an attack. The presumption is that until you have been a part of the organization for a while, you can't possibly understand it well enough to make constructive criticisms. Many people don't want newcomers to make changes until they understand and respect the existing system and all the work that has gone into it. Only then will your manager or coworkers be willing to entertain your suggestions for improvement.

Avoid "big splash" strategies

Conventional wisdom says that you need to show your new organization how smart and talented you are by using a "big splash" approach. So your natural tendency may be to charge ahead, trying to make big contributions and dreaming up great ideas to impress your colleagues. The problem is that if you do that before you have earned acceptance and before you understand your new organization well, you will most likely only embarrass yourself. The quickest way to make a "big splash" is to have the maturity not to try. You may think you know how to make a good impression, but experience says that you may be better off to wait a while.

Admitting what you don't know is more important than showing what you do know

What makes the most positive impression is not showing how much you know but rather having the maturity to know how much you don't know. That means keeping your eyes and ears open at first to find out as much as you can about the company and the people in it. You need to learn the ropes, to understand the nuances of how work gets done before you can have any hope of making intelligent suggestions for change or gaining new acceptance of your ideas. You might have an idea for the best new product design the organization will ever see, but you can't sell it to your coworkers and managers until you understand how the organization works. Managers know that college has given you only part of what you need to be successful. So don't make the mistake of believing that you are ready when you start.

Conformance may be more important than individuality

Being accepted generally requires more conformity to the organization's rules, norms, and ways of doing business than you might expect. As a new employee, you don't earn acceptance by challenging the system—you earn it by fitting in. In time you will have plenty of opportunities to develop your own style, assert some individuality, and make your job fit you better. For instance, during your first year you will probably be assigned to a team project that requires frequent meetings. Let's say that you are not the type of person who likes to work in groups. A typical strategy would be to quickly let the team know your preference for working alone. Since you'd still be considered a newcomer, such efforts would likely be interpreted by the team as a sign of new-graduate immaturity. A smarter strategy would be to operate the team's way until you have demonstrated the contributions you can make and are more accepted by the team members. Then suggest that you could do even more if you worked alone some of the time. The team will be much more receptive at that point.

Build a track record

The old saying is true: Nothing sells like success. Look for opportunities to be successful. You don't necessarily have to make home runs, just solid base hits. Be sure to make the right mistakes—that is, those that come naturally from learning, not those that come from immaturity and impatience. Become known for your dependability, your willingness to work hard, your ability to fit in, and your professional maturity. By doing so, you'll get on the "success spiral" quickly.

Six

Step 4: Manage the Impressions You Make

As a new hire, you must place a premium on managing the impressions you make in your first year. Realize that everything you do or say is being watched more closely during this period. As one manager we interviewed said, "You're really in a fishbowl right now. Whenever you start any job, I don't care what it is, there are a lot of people watching you and trying to assess your ability to succeed." Those people include your peers, subordinates, and bosses. Therefore, your goal is to be noticed for positive behavior and not behavior considered unacceptable by your organization.

Pity the graduates who carry their college student ways into the workplace. They get labeled early as "green," "immature," and "needing time to grow up." They don't get the good early opportunities and may be relegated to lesser tasks. You can't escape the fact that those who make the best early impressions will be the first to be given opportunities to succeed on projects that really matter and have the highest visibility.

Everything you do early on will be magnified in its impact. As you progress in your career and build a good professional reputation, your track record will provide a safety net to help protect you against inevitable mistakes and interpersonal gaffes. But in the first year you have no track record, so the impressions and perceptions others have of you really count. Even the smallest mistakes are magnified in impact when you're new.

It is hard to define precisely what the "right" impression is because every organization is different. That's why the first challenge in making a good impression is having the professional maturity to figure out what the organization wants to see. Steps 1–3 laid the groundwork for this step because a good attitude, realistic expectations, and strong breaking-in skills will immediately make a good impression. These really stand out in a new graduate. And they help you open up to learn exactly what makes a good impression.

Since your colleagues won't know you well in the beginning, your second challenge is to pay attention to the actions that create strong, positive first impressions. Little things that you don't think are very important can create impressions and perceptions. Often, they provide the only information that people can use to make early judgments about you. For example, volunteering to help on a project, paying attention in meetings, or taking manuals home to learn your job mean more than you might think. Make the right impressions and your colleagues will say, "She has potential," "He seems bright," or "That person looks like a good new hire." They'll want to associate with you, get to know you better, and help you. That's getting on the success spiral. Make the wrong impressions and they will say, "He's just another immature college grad," "She's going to have to grow up some more," or "Too bad we hired another one of *those* kind." They'll avoid you and your career may take an unexpected and unpleasant detour.

The third challenge is to remember that what's acceptable for more experienced people to do may not be okay for you to do. Avoid anything that reminds people of student-type behavior. At one organization, a dozen interns used to go to lunch together every day; they walked down the hall laughing and having a good time—until they realized that their behavior looked like a fraternity party to others. Another new hire started complaining about the way certain work was being done (and her opinions were valid) soon after being hired—until she realized that she was being viewed as a complainer. One recent graduate loved to wear crazy ties and was pleased to see other people doing it too—until he realized that people remembered him for his ties, not his ideas.

You should evaluate everything you do as to how it will look to people who know nothing about you but will form opinions about you. For the first year, be very conservative. Find opportunities to make a good impression by doing what you know people will like to see so you get "good" labels early. Avoid doing anything that could be misinterpreted. Remember, it's a lot easier to get noticed for the wrong choices you make than the right choices. After you earn acceptance, respect, and credibility, you probably can relax a bit and develop your personal work style.

Seven

Step 5: Build Effective Relationships

Picture a typical new graduate: sitting alone in his or her office, working long hours to meet a project deadline, taking manuals and books home at night to learn more, skipping lunch to make sure the work is done just right. If this sounds like a smart new graduate to you, you're only partially right. Organizations aren't just collections of tasks and duties but are people working together for a common goal. People shape an organization, determine how work gets done, decide your future, and determine the success of the organization. Every job, no matter how technical, requires being successful at working with, through, and around people. Focusing too hard on your work tasks leads you to ignore this equally important part of organizational life—building relationships with people.

In addition, the only way you will learn how to become successful in an organization is through interaction with people. Much of what you need to know about office procedures, the company's culture, and how to sell your ideas is not written down. It can be learned only from other people in the organization. It then follows that building good relationships is the only way that you can be successful in your job. If you don't build strong relationships—where people like you and want to teach you and help you—we can almost guarantee that you will not become an outstanding performer.

Here are some tips on how to build effective relationships at work.

Make building good working relationships a priority

Take the time to develop relationships with as many people as possible. Make this a priority on your to-do list. Get out of your office. Meet people, go to lunch with them, have coffee with them, and *listen*! Listening is a much more powerful relationship builder than talking. Don't forget to include secretaries and support staff. They can be instrumental in accomplishing your tasks. If you are introverted, force yourself to get to know your colleagues.

Understand what working relationships are

You don't have to become social friends to be good colleagues. Work relationships are different from social relationships. You may have become accustomed to associating only with people whom you like on a personal level. But you'll now have to build good working relationships with people who, frankly, you may not want to socialize with outside of the office or even invite to lunch. Or you may have to work well with people much older than you and with whom you have little in common. It is quite easy to be able to work well together even if you do not relate well on a personal level.

Develop good communication and relationship-building skills

Learn to communicate and work well with all types of people. Work on negotiating differences, avoiding or managing conflict, and seeing others' perspectives. Consider taking a course in interpersonal communication skills so you can understand your communication style and how to interact with people who use other styles. Learn to respect and work with all types of people.

Learn to work in teams

You cannot succeed by yourself. Just about everything you do will require you to team with others. No one person has all the expertise, information, and experience needed. College is a much more solitary pursuit than work. Being a team player means learning to share your success, involve others, become less competitive and possessive about your ideas, and be open to others' ideas.

Network, network, network

The old adage really is true: Who you know is just as important as what you know. Build a network of contacts, resources, advisers, and sources of information. Take advantage of opportunities to attend social functions, meetings, or seminars where you can meet colleagues. And don't limit yourself to people within your organization. Consider joining professional groups where you can meet outsiders too. They can help in the areas of information, perspective, resources, and, in today's turbulent times, future job changes.

Find a mentor, coach, or sponsor

Every new employee needs the guidance of more senior colleagues. If a structured mentoring program is available in your company, take advantage of it! If not, seek out older, more experienced employees who seem to have an interest in helping you. Listen carefully to their advice, even if you don't like it. Be careful to choose people who seem to be respected in the organization. Don't expect them to help you climb the corporate ladder (that's up to you) but just to help you learn. Find several mentors if one person doesn't totally fill the bill.

Eight

Step 6: Become a Good Follower

Your boss is the most important person on your first job. He or she will be largely responsible for providing opportunities for you to showcase your talents, seeing that you receive the training you need, setting the tone of your first year, shaping the organization's opinion and evaluation of you, determining your advancement beyond the entry position, and socializing you to the organization's culture. You must therefore give top priority to learning how to build a positive and mutually productive relationship with your boss.

Working for a boss is unlike any other relationship you have had. The problem is, you haven't been taught how to be an effective follower/employee. Just as there is a well-defined set of skills you can learn to be a manager, so too is there a well-defined set of skills for being a good follower. Colleges usually focus on developing future leaders, but you can't be a good leader until you first learn to be a good follower. Employers don't want to see your leadership skills in the beginning; they want to see your followership skills.

The success of your relationship with your boss is just as much your responsibility as it is your boss's. Don't slip into the "oughta-be" trap. For example, many new graduates think their boss "oughta-be" more available to spend time with them, but he or she simply can't due to work demands. Your boss might "oughta-be" doing lots of things differently or better (so you think). A bad boss is not a legitimate excuse for poor performance. Make it work or you may not advance. Ultimately, only you and your career will get hurt if your relationship doesn't work well.

First, you need to learn good follower skills that will allow you to be productive and effective in working with your manager. These skills will help insure that you give your manager what he or she needs. Talk to your colleagues and perhaps your boss to have these key questions answered:

- How much information does your boss like to have?

- Does your boss like to get regular updates or just know about problems?

- Does your boss like to be offered solutions to problems or be part of the problem-solving process?

- What are your boss's standards for quality work?

- What is your boss's agenda—wants, needs, and expectations?

- What can you to do to make your boss look good?

- How can you best support your boss?

- How hard does your boss expect you to work?

- What are the key demands on your boss's time?

- What are the critical resources you can help your boss obtain or conserve?

- How can you help your boss be more efficient and productive?

- When do you need to be most available?

- How can you make yourself indispensable?

Second, you need skills that make you an easy employee to manage. Practicing these skills can help your manager give you what you need to develop as a subordinate. Focus on the following:

- Which decisions does your boss like to make, and which ones will he or she delegate?

- In what way is your boss most comfortable giving you feedback?

- In which areas is it particularly important that you stay flexible?

- How much ownership of your job does your boss like to see?

- How independent does your boss like you to be?

- When does your boss like and need direct, honest answers?

- If you disagree with your boss, how should you handle this?

- What is the best way to get help from your boss if you need it?

- When your boss makes requests or gives instructions, what should you do to exceed his or her expectations?

- How should you respond when you are given an assignment?

Listen to this manager: "Once you get settled in and you know what your assignment is, be creative. Start thinking, What can I do that I have not been asked to do? What responsibilities could I take on that no one else seems to care about and make the boss happy that I took the initiative?" Remember, your boss wants you to be successful. After all, the quality of your work is a reflection on him or her as well.

Nine

Step 7: Understand Your Organization's Culture

Every company has its own unique personality or "culture," also known as the "around-hereisms" you'll hear every day: "We don't do things like that around here," "We like to see people working hard around here," "The boss likes people to show up early in the morning around here," and so on. These rules and norms, many of which are unspoken and informal, will shape everything you do in an organization from how you work with people to what you wear to work. Culture defines how you do what you were hired to do. How well you come to understand the culture will have a major impact on your first-year success.

Employers want employees who "fit" their organization's culture and enthusiastically embrace it. This doesn't mean that everyone should be a clone, but every organization has allowable limits of individuality. Generally, you shouldn't deviate too much from the norm until you are accepted as part of the team and have a track record of proven performance. Even new CEOs have failed when they changed companies because they didn't understand the power of organizational culture. If you don't take time to understand the culture, you are almost assured of making many dumb and embarrassing mistakes that will hurt your career.

Here are some critical elements of culture that you should pay attention to:

- Mission of the organization

- Guiding philosophies

- Basic values and norms

- Behavioral expectations

- Work ethic

- What gets rewarded

- Social norms

- Management philosophies

- Ethical standards

- Sacred beliefs and events

- Attitudes of employees

- Communication norms

- Work norms

- Office climate

Here are some examples of how not understanding the organization's culture can hurt you. Paula was a new hire who was quick to criticize a project only to find out that it was originally proposed by one of her senior managers, who still believed in it. John (in the opening scenario) failed because he didn't understand how important being a team player was. Mike, a new marketing representative, didn't understand that an office protocol was never to discuss an issue with your boss's boss without first informing your boss. Imagine his surprise when he was reprimanded for "going over his boss's head." Julie, a management trainee, didn't realize that not attending Friday evening socials was considered an insult to company management.

How do you learn culture? It's hard because it is rarely written down and most people can't directly explain it to you. But every employee is living it daily, so you learn it by observing it. Pay attention to "the way things are done around here." Watch your colleagues. What are they paying attention to and spending their time on? Learn what the norms and values of the organization are by watching how others behave. Find out what the basic mission and philosophy of the organization is by asking. Understand what people expect of you, particularly regarding the accepted work ethic and social norms. Pay attention to the political climate and how people communicate and work together.

All of this and more are part of the organization's culture. To be successful, you must take time to learn it before getting too adventurous. In chapter 16, you'll find a process for learning culture that is easy to implement. Don't let the culture you come from (education) distort your learning of the new culture.

Ten

Step 8: Adapt to the Organizational System

Adapting to the organizational system means learning how an organization really functions. Let's look at some important aspects of it.

Organizational politics—"Politics" is not a dirty word

Everything that happens in an organization includes politics. Politics is just the way business gets done when people work together. It can be nasty and vicious but usually is not. It is the process of sharing resources, sharing power, and influencing others.

The first rule for new graduates is not to get involved in "playing" politics. As a new employee, you lack the experience, clout, and skill to do it well. The second rule is to get rid of your political naiveté and consider the political aspects of everything you do. Use these four questions for starters:

- How will what you are working on affect others?

- Who else cares about what you are doing?

- Whom do you need on your side to accomplish the results you need?

- Who is against what you are working on?

The third rule is to use the first year to learn good organizational political skills. These include

- compromising with others

- involving others in decisions—before they are made

- understanding the "players" in every activity

- negotiating effectively

- understanding which battles are worth fighting and which ones are futile

- building coalitions of people who agree with you on an issue

- not "going out on a limb" by yourself

- identifying the controversial political issues

- understanding who has the power and who wants it

Think of politics in terms of playing with poker chips: you get some and you spend some. Use your first year to build your chips through good performance, helping others, and staying out of controversial political situations. Spend them later when you know how to do so wisely.

Organizational realities

Not only are organizations political, but they are often illogical, are sometimes unfair, make the wrong decisions, are slow to do things, don't always welcome change, aren't always fun, and sometimes don't like newcomers. Not all people in organizations are nice, helpful, or motivated. Simply put, they aren't perfect. You have to accept and adjust to these realities because they are true in every organization. You can still be happy and successful. Mature professionals are realistic and accept such imperfection.

Getting results

Organizations establish elaborate formal structures, systems, and procedures, but the people in them develop their own informal structures and methods that are often the way business really gets done. These are the "backdoor" ways of finding information, the shortcuts around the cumbersome accounting system, the informal agreements among departments to make work flow more quickly. Thousands of procedures and ways of doing things also exist that are never documented and simply evolve over time. These informal, unwritten ways of doing business make organizations more productive. If you want to get results in your job, you will have to master them. Don't get bogged down in the "official" procedures. Learn how work "really gets done around here." The only way to do that is to watch people, ask questions, and depend on other people to teach you.

Eleven

Step 9: Understand Your New-Hire Role

Nobody really likes being new in an organization. It can be uncomfortable and frustrating. However, all of your colleagues once had to adjust to the role of the newcomer, so they expect you to do the same. What we're suggesting is a new way of thinking: practicing the art of being new. We have found that it's just as important to learn how to be new as it is to be experienced. The more you understand and accept being new, and the better you become at acting like and being a new employee, the quicker you can leave the new employee stage behind. This is totally contrary to traditional thinking, which says you need to stop acting like a new employee as quickly as possible. Effective new employees understand the importance of the transition period. They accept the newcomer role, understand the special "rules" for newcomers, and vigorously attack the tasks of learning about the organization and becoming accepted rather than avoiding them.

Here are a few of the guidelines you should follow as a newcomer.

Don't resist new employee "dues"

Every organization has certain tasks that new employees are saddled with. These are commonly called "rites of passage" or "paying your dues." In many organizations, new hires must do copying, filing, or errands. Sometimes you are assigned all the menial tasks on a project. Often you get the worst desk and office (or cubicle). Some places won't let you write your own memos or take the lead in a presentation until you've worked there for a while. Don't take it personally. Sometimes these are done as a little bit of hazing and sometimes they are done just because someone has to do the menial work. Everyone was once new and was also treated this way. If you resist or complain, you will only show your immaturity because this is a reality of organizational life that everyone else understands. They won't appreciate your failure to understand.

If you are treated this way, relax. Your opportunities will come. Remember, this is a transition period, not your entire career. We guarantee you that you will win much respect by fitting into your role, whatever it is or however trivial it may seem, and doing your work to the best of your ability as cheerfully as possible.

Understand the bigger picture

Many new graduates fail to learn about the big picture in their organization. They develop "tunnel vision," focusing only on their needs, their interests, and their jobs. When asked to do the copying for a big project due next week, they see it as an insult instead of their part in helping the department complete an important project. When the boss doesn't have much time to talk with them for a few weeks, they feel neglected instead of realizing that the boss has many other very important matters to attend to. When a training program is delayed or converted to on-the-job training, they become angry that they didn't get what was promised instead of looking at the drop in profitability that forced the vice president to cut the budget. And when colleagues don't take the time to help them, they feel shortchanged instead of volunteering to help with other important priorities.

Your first new job is probably very important to you and consumes most of your energy and time. However, your organization has many other priorities that are equally as important or more important than helping you do your job well. Look at the bigger picture. What might seem vitally important to you may not be as important to everyone else. Be professionally mature enough to recognize this and take responsibility for yourself.

Find your niche

It's frustrating when you are new and don't really have a well-defined role. We all like having a part to play and feeling that we can contribute. Look carefully at what role the people in your organization want you to play. Do they want you to be a loyal assistant but not have significant responsibility of your own for a while? Do they need you to step in and take over for someone who is out for major surgery, even though you may not feel ready? Do they want you to spend six months going to school and reading manuals?

Whatever they expect, your job is to match their schedule and their plan, not to follow just your own. Many new graduates create problems for themselves and for others by trying to force the organization to fit their own plans. Think about it. The time will come when you can push the system (probably about halfway through your first year) but only after you are accepted and respected. Until then, forget what *you* think your role should be and figure out what *the organization* wants your role to be. Then fill that role willingly and to the best of your ability. This happens so rarely that you will be admired and respected very quickly. Then you can pursue your agenda.

Twelve

Step 10: Develop Work Smarts

At this point in the twelve-step process, you will have begun to adjust your attitudes and expectations, learn how to break in, build the relationships you need, understand the organization, and learn how to work through the organization to get results. Now you are ready to become an outstanding performer. The next three steps focus more directly on task performance. Step 10 addresses one more set of generic skills, "work smarts." These involve learning how to apply your knowledge and to develop the professional skills necessary to accomplish your goals.

Applying your knowledge

Many new graduates find that they struggle when trying to apply their knowledge in a job setting. Book knowledge is fine, but what can you do with it? How does it fit the tasks you have to do? How can you use it to achieve results? What are the practical applications of what you know? For example, it's one thing to know the principles of designing a good training program but quite another to sit with a stack of reference materials and use the design principles to create an effective training program for your colleagues. Let your coworkers guide you in learning how to make your book knowledge useful.

Developing professional skills

You will need to develop numerous professional skills in order to perform your job. These include

- managing your time efficiently
- setting priorities
- juggling multiple projects
- writing memos, letters, and reports
- making oral presentations
- managing work flow
- managing and participating in meetings
- selling your ideas
- working with secretaries and office assistants
- organizing your work and office
- setting realistic deadlines
- meeting deadlines
- producing the right level of quality

Focus on developing these essential professional work skills. Talk to your organization's human resource department if you need help.

Thirteen

Step 11: Master the Tasks of Your Job

While the emphasis in this book has been on the nontask elements of your job, don't be fooled into thinking that task performance is not important. It is, in fact, essential. We have not spent much time on this aspect of your first job because most organizations are very good at teaching new employees the basic tasks of their jobs. Furthermore, few managers complain that new graduates don't master their basic job tasks.

When you have completed the previous ten steps, you will be in a position to really master the tasks of your job. You will fully understand these tasks, how they fit into the organization, how work really gets done, and whom to work with to accomplish the organization's goals. Now you simply have to master the tasks.

Your employer will most likely provide you with some training to get you started. Don't take it lightly. We think it's odd how many new graduates complain about the content of their "basic training" when they really don't have any idea what it is they need to learn. Assume the training is conducted the way it is for a reason and learn as much as you can.

Fourteen

Step 12: Acquire the Knowledge, Skills, and Abilities You Need

I f you are like most new graduates, you will find you lack certain skills and abilities that you need. Employers expect you to need development, so take advantage of the development opportunities you're offered, and don't be embarrassed to ask for training or help.

Take responsibility for your own development

As a professional, you have to take the responsibility and initiative to guide your own development. At this point, you should have a very good idea as to what type of development you need. Sit down with your manager and other colleagues and ask for their input. Listen to your performance reviews, particularly about where you may be lacking some skill or knowledge. Then devise a plan to guide your development.

Adopt a continual learning mind-set

If you have spare time, which often happens with new employees, use it to learn something new. Nobody will force you to develop like professors forced you to learn in college. It is your responsibility now. You can always find something new to learn and opportunities to increase your skills and knowledge of the organization. Many organizations have self-directed learning centers, where employees can choose a subject and learn at their own pace, or access optional training programs. If yours offers these benefits, use them. Or use technology-based learning (e.g., computer-based training, Internet courses) to acquire new skills. You cannot learn too much in your first year.

Fifteen

Taking Responsibility for Your First-Year Success

It is your responsibility to make your transition from college to the workplace a success, not your employer's. Good employers will help you, but if they don't, remember that excuses won't get you promoted. In college, you could complain to the dean or even the professor. But at work, nobody will care about your career like you. If you're not successful, you might be able to blame someone else, but your career will still suffer. Take the initiative and responsibility now!

Putting these twelve steps into practice takes some time and effort. Unfortunately, few jobs allow you to work through these steps one at a time. Instead, you'll be involved with all of them at once, at least to some degree. Use the steps to set priorities of what you need to learn. Steps 1–3 should be your first priority and can be accomplished (for the most part) before you start work or soon thereafter. Making the right impressions and building relationships with your boss and coworkers (steps 4–6) should be your next priority. Learning the culture, adapting to the organizational system, and understanding your role (steps 7–9) will follow naturally from your relationships. Finally, your task performance (steps 10–12) will be the next priority as you move along in your first year and people begin to look for a higher level of performance. While you will be performing at least basic job tasks from the beginning, most organizations will start you slowly, which will give you time to work on the other steps.

Each organization is a little different, so the priorities of the steps may have to be varied. For example, if you start work when the organization is trying to meet a major deadline, you may have to focus on tasks before you are ready and may not have time to build relationships. However, when the deadline is met, you'll need to backtrack since each of the twelve steps must be successfully accomplished. Do not skip any step.

Issues and Challenges

Many new graduates find the transition to work challenging. Here are some common issues that arise:

"The people I work with don't understand what it's like to be new"

This is probably true. It takes only a year or two in the workplace for someone to forget what it's like to be new. And few managers receive training in how to bring new employees into an organization. Don't expect anyone to automatically know what you need. Communicate your needs in a nondemanding way.

"Too much conformance is expected"

Remember two things: first, the advice in this book is just to get you started. You won't always have to conform as much as you're conforming now. Second, individuality may seem very important to you right now, but the work world generally requires more conformance than college.

"I'm not as happy as I thought I would be"

It is very common for new graduates to feel a little disappointed with their first jobs, usually because their expectations are not met. Often, there is a burst of happiness and enthusiasm in the beginning, followed by a letdown, and then—here's the good news—a return of enjoyment and satisfaction once the adjustment phase is past.

"I'm bored"

The first six months on a job may not be as challenging as you were expecting or are accustomed to. It will likely take time for you to grow into the level of responsibility and challenge you expected early in your career. For many, work is never quite as demanding as college was. Remember that it is difficult to find the constant high level of intellectual challenge you experienced in college anywhere else. However, work offers different types of challenges that can be just as rewarding when you meet them.

"I can't handle it all"

Yes, the opposite can happen when you get too much to do too fast and it all seems very confusing. Try to relax. Even the most experienced employees sometimes feel overwhelmed in a new job. It takes time to settle in, but the situation will get better as you learn the ropes. Don't be afraid to ask for help and don't expect more of yourself than everyone else does.

"I have a bad assignment"

Sometimes this does happen. Bad bosses, bad jobs, and budget cuts are all unfortunate realities. In most cases, the fastest way out of a bad situation is to do the best job possible under the circumstances. Turn to your mentor for advice. Usually "grin and bear it" will get you further than loud complaining because most of your colleagues have been in the same position at some point in their career. If the situation is intolerable, make sure you discuss it in a very professional and nonaccusatory way, focusing on the problem and your desired solution.

Sixteen

The Quick-Start Learning Tool

So far we have focused on what you need to learn. However, awareness is only part of your challenge. Equally challenging is the fact that most learning that occurs during your first year on the job will require fundamentally different skills than you cultivated in college. In other words, how you learn at work will be fundamentally different from the way you learned in college.

Here are some key differences you'll find in the workplace:

- Many skills and protocols can be learned only by interacting with other people in the organization, so *social learning* skills are most important.

- The learning process is usually an *experiential* one; learning occurs while you're engaged in work projects.

- *Self-directed learning* is the norm since you have to take the initiative to learn more than the task knowledge to do your job.

- The learning is *unstructured* in that it goes on all the time with no definite beginning and ending points.

- The learning is *indeterminate* in that it may be difficult to tell when you have the "right" answers or when learning is completed, especially when dealing with complex or unusual problems.

In short, learning is often an "unstructured," but continuous, process.

Contrast this to the learning model in college, which is predominantly book learning in formal classrooms led by instructors of neatly packaged courses. The skills for successful learning in college bear little resemblance to those needed in organizations. Unless you learn new ways to learn, you may have difficulty using the twelve-step process. Successful employees have developed the ability to learn in this new way.

The Quick-Start learning tool presented in the next section leads you through this new learning process. First, an interview protocol is presented that helps you engage in the kind of social learning process you will need to do lots more of. However, you will quickly see that the information you collect will be disorganized and sometimes hard to figure out how to use. Thus, appendix A includes worksheets to help you sort the information you collect into the twelve-step framework. Action-planning worksheets are also presented in appendix B to help you turn your new learning into action steps.

A word of warning: This process may feel very different from what you are accustomed to. Remember, learning how to be successful in an organization is a fundamentally different learning process. If you use the worksheets in this chapter, you will not only be learning what it takes to be successful in your new organization, you will also be learning how to learn in a whole new way. These learning skills will help you throughout your career as you move to new jobs, departments, or companies. The ability to learn in a different way can make a big difference in your career.

Quick-Start Learning Tool Overview

Because the new employee learning process may be unfamiliar to you, we have created the Quick-Start learning tool to help you. The tool has three components:

- *Interview Protocol*—a set of questions and instructions to guide you in interviewing your new colleagues to collect the information you need to successfully enter an organization.

- *Analysis Templates*—a set of worksheets to help you sort this information into the twelve steps described in this book.

- *Action Planning*—a set of worksheets to help you organize your thinking about areas in which you need to develop your skills.

Field tests of this tool have yielded great results. First, the simple act of asking people to tell you how to get started makes a great impression on them. Human resource directors typically believe employees will not devote any time to being interviewed, but our experience is the opposite—they love it. Second, with these interview questions you will learn in a few days what could take you a year to learn otherwise. Third, the questions and worksheets will start conversations between you and your colleagues or your boss that will provide enormously valuable coaching. Usually the coaching continues well past these interviews. Finally, you will learn how to learn about a new job. It is a great tool that works!

Not everyone uses this tool the same way—feel free to adapt its components to fit your personal style or situation. For example, some interview questions may not be relevant to your job or organization. Some people like to write down their thoughts on the worksheets, while others may prefer to use the worksheets as thought starters without actually writing down the answers. However you approach the process, you must complete all three steps: collect information about your new organization, analyze it to understand it within the twelve-step framework, and then plan your own development.

One of the best ways to start to use the worksheets is to initiate conversations with your boss. Many new employees have had great results by showing the boss (or colleagues) their completed worksheets. Their conversations have turned into wonderful coaching sessions because the tool provides a structured way to discuss issues that are sometimes sensitive. Also, many experienced employees have forgotten what new employees need to learn and the tool reminds them what they need to teach you.

Quick-Start Interview Protocol

The Quick-Start interview protocol should be implemented during your first six months as a new employee. The questions have been carefully planned and structured to help you learn important information about your employer. If the purpose of a question is not immediately clear, it will become clearer later during your first few months on the job.

As a new employee, you will be quite busy, but you should make it a priority to find time to complete the interviews. In some cases, you may not be able to get all of the information you ask for. That's okay as long as you make every effort you can to get the information.

Part I—Getting to Know People in the Organization

As discussed earlier, meeting, working with, understanding, and communicating with people is vitally important in the workplace. The first set of exercises is designed to get you started in that process by meeting and interviewing a few of the people in your new organization. When interviewing them, feel free to tell them that you are completing an exercise as part of your training. Most will be happy to help you.

Identify four to six people in your new organization who you would like to interview. They should be at different levels in the organization and represent a mixture of job functions. Be sure to include people in both management and nonmanagement positions and at least one person who is fairly new in the organization (five years or less). Identify your interviewees below including name and title.

_____

_____

_____

_____

_____

Schedule time with each person to discuss the subjects outlined below. Be sure to take careful notes so you can recall their answers later. Discuss anything you want, but be sure to cover the subjects on the interview guidelines. When scheduling an interview, be sure to explain the purpose of the session. You might use an introduction like this:

> I am meeting with four to six people to discuss various aspects of working at _____ [name of organization]. The information I am collecting will help me learn more about the organization. None of the questions are intended to be prying, and I hope none of the questions are offensive. If you are uncomfortable answering any of them, please let me know and we will eliminate those questions.

Use the following statements and questions to guide your interview:

- Discuss your general career history including education, jobs held, career paths, and so on.

- Discuss in more detail your career at _____ [name of organization]. How long have you been here? What have you been doing? Where do you see yourself in the future here?

- What has your tenure at _____ [name of organization] been like?

- What do you see as the rewards and challenges of working at _____ [name of organization]?

- What do you see as this organization's mission and basic values?

- How would you describe the daily work life at _____ [name of organization]?

- What professional characteristics do you feel are needed to be successful at _____ [name of organization]?

- If a new employee wants to make a positive first impression at _____ [name of organization], what should he or she do?

- What do new employees do that leaves the most negative impressions?

- What should a new employee expect during the first six months?

- What problems do you typically have (or see people having) with new employees?

- What attitudes are rewarded by the organization?

- What is the typical management style at _____ [name of organization]?

- What tips do you have for getting along well with one's boss at _____ [name of organization]?

- What are the best ways to really get to know the organization and how it really works?

- What are the most important things to know about getting work done in the organization?

- What should a new employee expect to be doing in the first few assignments in your division?

- What other people should a new employee get to know in the division?

- What advice would you give a new employee just starting out?

- What did you do when you were new with the organization that helped you get started on the right foot?

Part II—Getting to Know the Work Group

It is vitally important that you get to know the members of your new group as well as you possibly can. While this can take some time, you can speed up the process by taking the initiative to seek out information about the group members.

In this second part of the interviews, you'll get to know the specific group to which you will be initially assigned. If your assignment has not been finalized, then select any work group, preferably the one to which you think you're most likely to be assigned. Schedule time to meet with the manager of that group and several people who work within it. The purpose of the meetings is to learn as much as you can about that group and its work.

Use these questions to guide the interviews:

- How does the group's work relate to the overall mission of the organization?

- Where does the group fit in the organizational structure?

- Specifically, what is the group set up to do and why does it exist?

- What is the group's history?

- Describe the structure of the group and name each person in it. What does each person do?

- What projects is the group currently working on?

- What are the major challenges the group faces in completing these projects?

- What are the most rewarding parts of working on this group's projects?

- What is daily life like in this work group?

- What is the physical layout and location of the office like?

- What tasks would I likely be assigned as a new employee in the group?

- What would be expected of me if I joined this group?

- How could I be most helpful if I were to join the group?

- What does it take to receive an excellent evaluation?

- What skills or expertise should a person have to be successful?

- How would you describe the management style of the group's direct supervisor?

- When working with this supervisor, what steps should a person take to build a good working relationship?

- What are the relationships between the group members like? Do people work closely together or individually?

- How would they feel about having a new employee join their group?

- What kinds of policies, procedures, and operating rules should I know in order to work effectively in this group and in this division?

Conclusion

Get on the "Success Spiral"

Once you accept the unique nature of the transition from college to work, this period can be lots of fun, very exciting, and a terrific start to a successful career. The twelve steps discussed in this book will help you make sense of a very critical career stage, build a solid foundation for advancement, and get a fast start. Most important, they will keep you from making dumb mistakes and thereby spoiling years of hard work and missing the rewards you have earned. Is this period easy? No, not for everyone. But most new graduates conclude by the end of the first year that it was worth it.

The advice given here represents a conservative, safe approach to starting a career. Most graduates have told us that as they got to know their new organizations, they found areas where they didn't have to be so conservative. Each of them reported something a little different about his or her organization, but nobody has ever said he or she made mistakes with this approach. The twelve-step process will keep you out of trouble in the beginning and put you on the road to a professionally mature image right from the start. No employer will fault you for a conservative start.

If approached correctly, this can be a wonderful time in your professional life. Have fun, work hard, enjoy your success, and good luck!

Appendix A

Quick-Start Learning Templates

You will find that the Quick-Start interview will yield a great deal of information, but you may wonder how to use all of it. To help you organize the information and to help you plan your development, a series of learning templates is provided in this appendix. These templates will help you sort the information you gather into twelve "buckets" corresponding with the twelve steps in the book.

The following pages contain abbreviated versions of worksheets. For some people, these will be sufficient, but others may want complete worksheets. Complete worksheets can be downloaded from our Web site: www.NewEmployeeSuccess.com.

Attitudes

In the left column, list success-related attitudes that you have observed and been told about in your organization. Then give yourself a grade (A–F) on each of them. (Be honest!) Finally, identify some possible improvement strategies.

Success Attitude	My Grade	Improvement Strategies

Expectations

Most new employees find that few of the expectations they had before they joined the organization exactly match what they experience on the job. Some expectations are exceeded, but some are not met. Regardless, it is important to identify how your actual experience has matched your previous expectations.

Think back to the time period just before you joined this organization. List at least five expectations you had about this organization and job. Then, for each of them, indicate with a "+" or a "–" whether your experience has been better ("+") or worse ("–") than expected. Be sure to include both types.

Expectation	+/–

1. For each of the expectations you had that were not met, consider how these unmet expectations have affected your work. List any ways you think of.

2. If you were asked to go back to your college campus and talk to graduating seniors about coming to work here, what would you tell them are the five "myths" they ought to be sure to forget if they want to have a good and successful experience here?

Breaking In

Breaking in to an organization is a unique time that requires you to use special strategies in order to become accepted, respected, and productive quickly. Unfortunately, few people recognize the importance and uniqueness of this period.

1. List the words you would use to describe what it feels like for you to be new in this organization.

2. What have been the major issues/frustrations for you while breaking in?

3. List at least three specific steps you have taken as a new employee to help you get off to a fast start.

4. List at least three steps that you think will help you earn the respect of the people in this organization.

Impression Management

When first joining an organization, the impressions you make are just as important as your actual performance.

1. Identify at least three instances in which you think you have been able to make a *positive* impression. Describe each.

2. Identify at least three instances in which you think something you did or said made a *negative* impression. Describe each.

3. Identify at least five ways you can make a positive impression quickly in this organization.

4. List at least three steps you can take to avoid making a negative impression.

Relationships

People are just as important as tasks in an organization. You cannot succeed by yourself, so a priority must be placed on building effective working relationships at all levels in the organization.

List at least five groups of people who you think are important to your success in the organization. Then for each, list specific steps you have taken or can take to build good working relationships with them. Be sure to include peers, support staff, other members of your work group, resource networks, senior management, and anybody else who helps you get your job done and be successful.

Person/Group	Strategy

Followership

While you're a new employee, your boss is the single most important person to you. Thus, your relationship with your boss is critical to your career success. Before you can ever be a good leader, you must learn to be a good follower.

1. List at least three skills you think are needed to be a good subordinate.

2. List five ways you can demonstrate good followership skills in your organization.

3. List at least three specific expectations your boss has of you as a subordinate.

4. List below the action steps you should take and actions you should avoid to build an excellent working relationship with your boss:

Do	Avoid

Organizational Culture

List what you have learned about each of these culture elements from your interviews:

1. Mission of the organization

2. Guiding philosophies

3. Basic values and norms

4. Behavioral expectations

5. Work ethic

6. What gets rewarded

7. Social norms

8. Management philosophies

9. Ethical standards

10. Sacred beliefs and events

11. Attitude of employees

12. Communication norms

13. Work norms

14. Office climate

Organizational Savvy

One of the most important and difficult tasks of breaking in to an organization is learning what it *really* takes to be successful. In the left column, list at least five critical factors for success in your organization. Then in the right column, write specific strategies you are currently using to demonstrate those factors to management.

Success Factors	Strategies

Roles

An essential task for all new employees is finding their proper role in the organization and understanding where they fit in the larger picture. This role-definition process is sometimes difficult and time consuming. Unfortunately, the role in which you are placed seldom matches the role you'd prefer. Understanding your role and adapting to it are essential tasks.

1. Describe your role as a new employee in your organization.

2. List at least five expectations you think your organization has of you in this role.

3. Describe what you would like your role to be.

Work Smarts

One of the important aspects of being successful is to be an outstanding performer. You will need to develop professional skills in order to perform your job.

1. For each skill listed below, grade yourself A to F on how well you think you manage these critical aspects of being a star performer. (Be honest!)

   - Managing time efficiently
   - Setting priorities
   - Juggling multiple projects
   - Writing memos, letters, and reports
   - Making oral presentations
   - Managing work flow

- Managing and participating in meetings
- Selling ideas
- Using good telephone skills
- Working with a secretary
- Organizing my work and office
- Setting realistic deadlines
- Meeting deadlines
- Producing the right level and quality
- Motivating myself

2. For those skills rated lower than A, arrange a professional development opportunity within the next year to achieve the desired skill level. Ask for feedback from your supervisor on specific areas in question.

Tasks of Your Job

A job includes many activities and tasks. However, usually only a small subset are really important to your success. List below the *core* tasks of your job. These should be the tasks in which it is absolutely essential for you to show strong results because they are important to the organization. Now, in the right column, list the result that is expected of you on each task.

Core Job Task	Result Expected

Knowledge, Skills, and Abilities

More than likely, you will need to acquire new knowledge, skills, or abilities to complete your job tasks at the level required. Answer the questions below to plan your learning.

1. What knowledge, skills, or abilities do you not have now but need to develop to achieve the results required in your current job?

2. What knowledge, skills, or abilities do you have but need to become more proficient in to achieve the results required in your current job?

3. What knowledge, skills, or abilities do you not have now but need to develop for your next job assignment?

4. Where can you get the training you need?

Appendix B

Quick-Start Personal Action Plan

Strategies

This worksheet will help you identify strategies to address each problem area identified in the Quick-Start learning templates.

1. In the first column, circle the name of each step you circled in the Quick-Start learning templates.

2. In the second column, write at least one or two goals for improvement.

3. In the third column, write at least three strategies you can use to address the problem you have identified.

Step	Goals for Improvement	Strategies

Resources and Barriers

1. List any resources (e.g., people, training, information) you will need to accomplish your goals. Be specific.

2. What barriers or problems (if any) do you anticipate that you may have to work around in accomplishing your goals?

Index

A

acceptance, earning, 11–12, 22
applying your knowledge, 46–47
asking for help, 55
attitudes
    accepting bad assignments/situations, 56
    change, readiness for, 16
    confidence, 16
    humility, 14–15
    learning, readiness for, 15
    longer-term perspective, 17
    open-mindedness, 16–17
    positive, 18
    respect for others, 16
    work ethic, 17
Attitudes template, 70

B

bad work assignments, 56
barriers, listing, 79
bigger picture, understanding the, 43–44
"big splash" approach, 22
boredom, 55

bosses, 32–35
Breaking In template, 71
building good relationships, 29

C

career-building, 26
challenges
    avoiding student-type behavior, 27
    expectations of job, 20
    of transitioning from college to work, 54–56
    work versus college, 10
change, readiness for, 16
changing the system, 22
coaching relationships, 31
college versus work. See work versus college
communication skills, 30, 54
company culture, 36–38
complaining, 18
confidence, 16
conforming to the company, 23, 55
confusion, 55
conservative approach, 67–68

Index

continual learning mind-set, 52,
    58
credibility, earning, 11–12
culture, company, 36–38

D
dependability, 24
development, guiding your own,
    41–52
direction, receiving, 9
dues, paying your, 43

E
elements of company culture,
    36–37
expectations, adjusting your, 19–
    20, 55
Expectations template, 70

F
feedback, 9
first year
    developing abilities, 10–11
    goals of, 11–12
    impact of on your future,
        4–5
    as transition stage, 3–4
fitting in, company culture and,
    36–37
Followership template, 73
follower skills, 32–35

G
goals, 11–12, 13, 24–26
guidelines for newcomers,
    43–45

H
help, asking for, 55
humility, 14–15

I
immaturity, 5
Impression Management tem-
    plate, 71–72
impressions, making the right,
    25–27
indeterminate learning, 58
initiative, taking, 35

K
knowledge, applying your,
    46–47
Knowledge, Skills, and
    Abilities template, 77

L
learning. See also Quick-Start
    Learning Tool
    company's culture, 38
learning, *continued*
    continual, 15, 52
    types of self-, 58
longer-term perspective, 17

M
maturity, 22, 23
mentor relationships, 31
mind-set, continual learning, 52
mistakes, 10, 38, 67

N
negative attitude, 18
networking, 30
new-hire role, 42
niche, finding your, 44–45
nontask components of jobs, 10

O
open-mindedness, 16–17
organization, understanding the
    company's, 22

organizational culture, 36–38, 41

Organizational Culture template, 73–74

Organizational Savvy template, 74

organizational system, adapting to, 39–41

outsider feelings, 21

P

paying your dues, 43

people, getting to know, 61–64

performance, 11, 33

Personal Action Plan, 78–79

politics, organizational, 39–41

positive attitude, 18

potential, 16

pride, 14–15, 16

process of learning. See Quick-Start Learning Tool

professional behavior, 10

professional development, your, 51

professional skills, 47–48

Q

Quick-Start Learning Tool
differences between work and college, 57–59
Interview Protocol, 60–66
overview of, 59–60
templates, 70–77

Quick-Start Personal Action Plan, 78–79

R

relationships
building good, 28
communication skills, 29
mentor/sponsor/coach, 31
networking, 30
overview, 28–29

relationaships, *continued*
teamwork, 30
working versus social, 29–30
with your boss, 32–33

Relationships template, 72

reputation, building a professional, 26

resources, listing, 79

respect, earning, 11–12

respect for others, 16

responsibilities, your, 51–52, 53–56

results, getting, 41

role as new hire, 42–45

Roles template, 74

rules
avoiding politics, 39–40
learning new, 3–4
for newcomers, 42–43

S

Schein, Edgar, 4

self-directed learning, 58

skills
being a manageable employee, 34–35
being new, 42–43
breaking in, 21–24
communication, 30, 54
communication/relationship building, 30
developing professional, 47–48
follower, 32–35
getting results, 41
organizational politics, 39–41
"playing" politics, 39–40
professional, 47–48
task-related knowledge and, 11, 49–50

work, 47–48
social relationships versus
    working, 29–30
sponsor relationships, 31
strategies
    conformance, 23
    Quick-Start Learning Tool,
        69–77
    Quick-Start Personal
        Action Plan, 78–79
success, 24, 53–56
"success spiral," 4, 67–68

T

tact/diplomacy, 9
task-related knowledge/skills,
    11, 49–50
Tasks of Your Job template, 76
teamwork, 30
templates for Quick-Start
    Learning Tool
    Attitudes, 70
    Breaking In, 71
    Expectations, 70–71
    Followership, 73
    Impression Management,
        71–72
    Knowledge, Skills, and
        Abilities, 77
    Organizational Culture,
        73–74
    Organizational Savvy, 74

    Relationships, 72
    Roles, 75
    Tasks of Your Job, 76
    Work Smarts, 75–76
track records, building, 24
training, 9, 50
transitions, college to work, 2
"tunnel vision," 43–44
twelve-step process overview, 2–
    3, 12–13

U

unstructured learning, 58

W

work ethic, 17
work groups, getting to know,
    64–66
working relationships versus
    social, 29
work skills, 47–48
"work smarts," 46–48
Work Smarts template, 75–76
work style, developing your, 27
work versus college
    attitudes, 14–18
    difference in processes of
        each, 6–7
    failing to recognize
        differences, 9–10
    key differences between, 8,
        57–59

Related Books

Helping Your New Employee Succeed: Tips for Managers of New College Graduates, Elwood F. Holton III and Sharon S. Naquin

This book is the perfect guide for supervisors of new college graduates. The twelve-part new employee development model is used to teach supervisors and managers what they need to teach new employees. In most organizations, the manager or supervisor of a new employee is perhaps the most important person in creating a successful transition from college to the workplace. The manager either has direct control over many of the twelve transition tasks or can create successful learning opportunities for the ones they don't control. Yet few managers have been taught how to help a new employee enter an organization even though the potential costs of not doing it right are considerable. Furthermore, most managers have worked long enough to have forgotten what a new employee experiences. In today's labor markets, retention of key talent is essential. This book helps supervisors know what new employees experience and what they need to be taught to successfully acclimate to the organization.

So You're New Again: How to Succeed When You Change Jobs, Elwood F. Holton III and Sharon S. Naquin

This book is targeted at new employees with prior work experience who are making significant transitions into new workplaces. These "new" employees could be ones changing companies or ones making significant changes within an organization (e.g., transferring between departments). The twelve-part new employee development model is again used but with a special focus on issues that experienced professionals encounter. Considerable emphasis is placed on the *unlearning* process. For experienced employees, the biggest issues are often not in knowing what to learn but in being able to unlearn and let go of old ways of doing business. Each development task in the twelve-part model teaches them what they must learn *and* what they must unlearn to make a successful transition.

About the Authors

Elwood F. Holton III, Ed.D., is a professor of human resource development (HRD) at Louisiana State University, where he also coordinates the HRD programs and serves as executive director of the Center for Leadership Development. He is also the im-mediate past president of the Academy of Human Resource Development. He consults with public, private, and nonprofit organizations on all types of human resource development, leadership development, and performance improvement projects. Holton has developed and refined his twelve-step model through numerous presentations to new employee and human resource practitioner groups, including consulting engagements in organizations such as J. P. Morgan, Enterprise Rent-A-Car, the U.S. Department of Energy, the U.S. General Services Administration, and the Multiple Sclerosis Society. He is the author of 11 books and more than 150 articles.

Sharon S. Naquin, Ph.D., is the director of the Office of Human Resource Development Research and an assistant professor of human resource development at Louisiana State University. She has eleven years of experience in corporate human resources. In those roles, she has recruited, hired, and trained hundreds of new employees. As a consultant, she has worked on all types of human resource, employee training, and performance improvement problems. She has also published in the areas of dispositional effects on adult learning in the workplace, organizational needs analysis, leadership development, performance improvement systems, community workforce development systems, and management development evaluation.